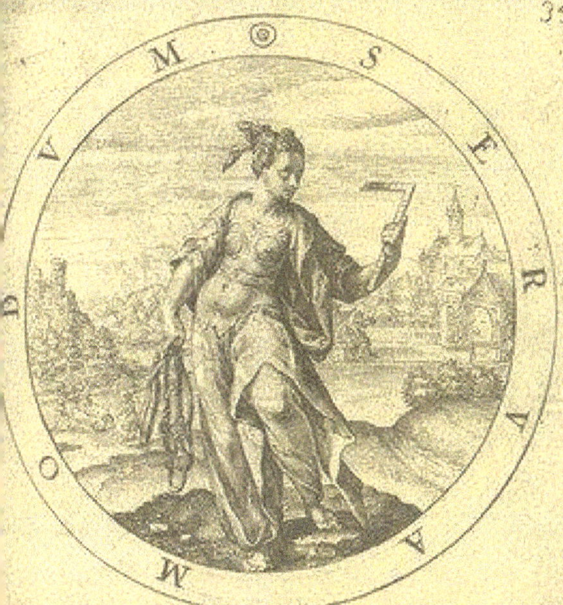

Mens SERVARE MODUM, rebus sufflata secundis,
Nescit, & affectus frena tenere sui

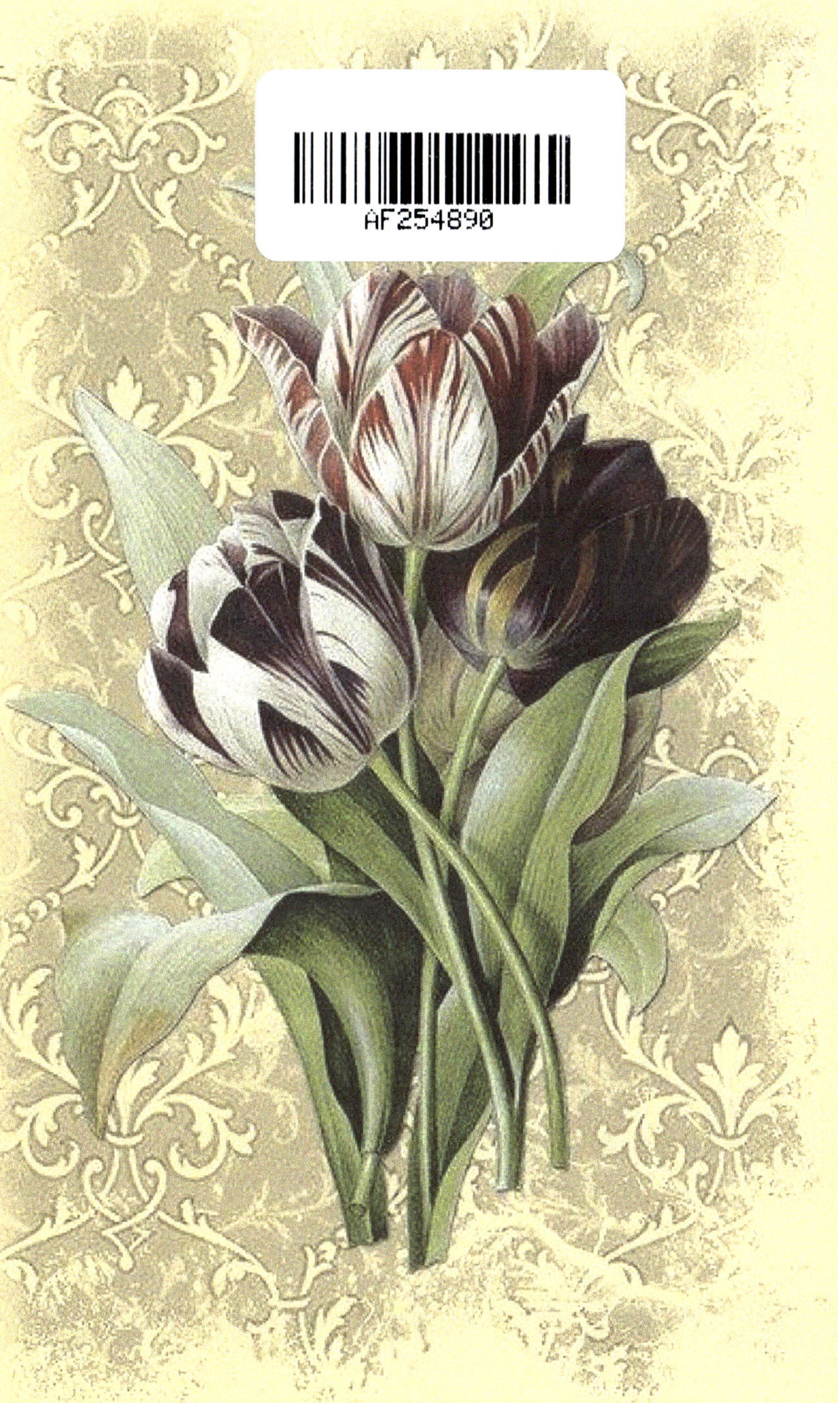

Adieu.

In every flake that flies,
Withering wandering skies,
    For a sigh — Farewell, Adieu?

Sinking suffering heart
That know'st how weary thou art—
    Soul so fain for a flight,—
Aye, spread your wings to depart,
Sad soul and sorrowing heart,—
    Adieu, Farewell, Goodnight.

DVM · O · SERVA · MODVM · A · M

Mens servare modum, rebus sufflata secundis,
Nescit, & affectus fræna tenere sui.

Adieu.

Waving whispering trees,
What do you say to the breeze?
    And what says the breeze to you?
And passing winds all the while,
Murmuring murmuring trees,
    Would ye sigh forever an Adieu?

Sighing turbulent seas,
Winds that wrestle with these,
    Echo heard in the wild,—
And fleeting life ill at ease

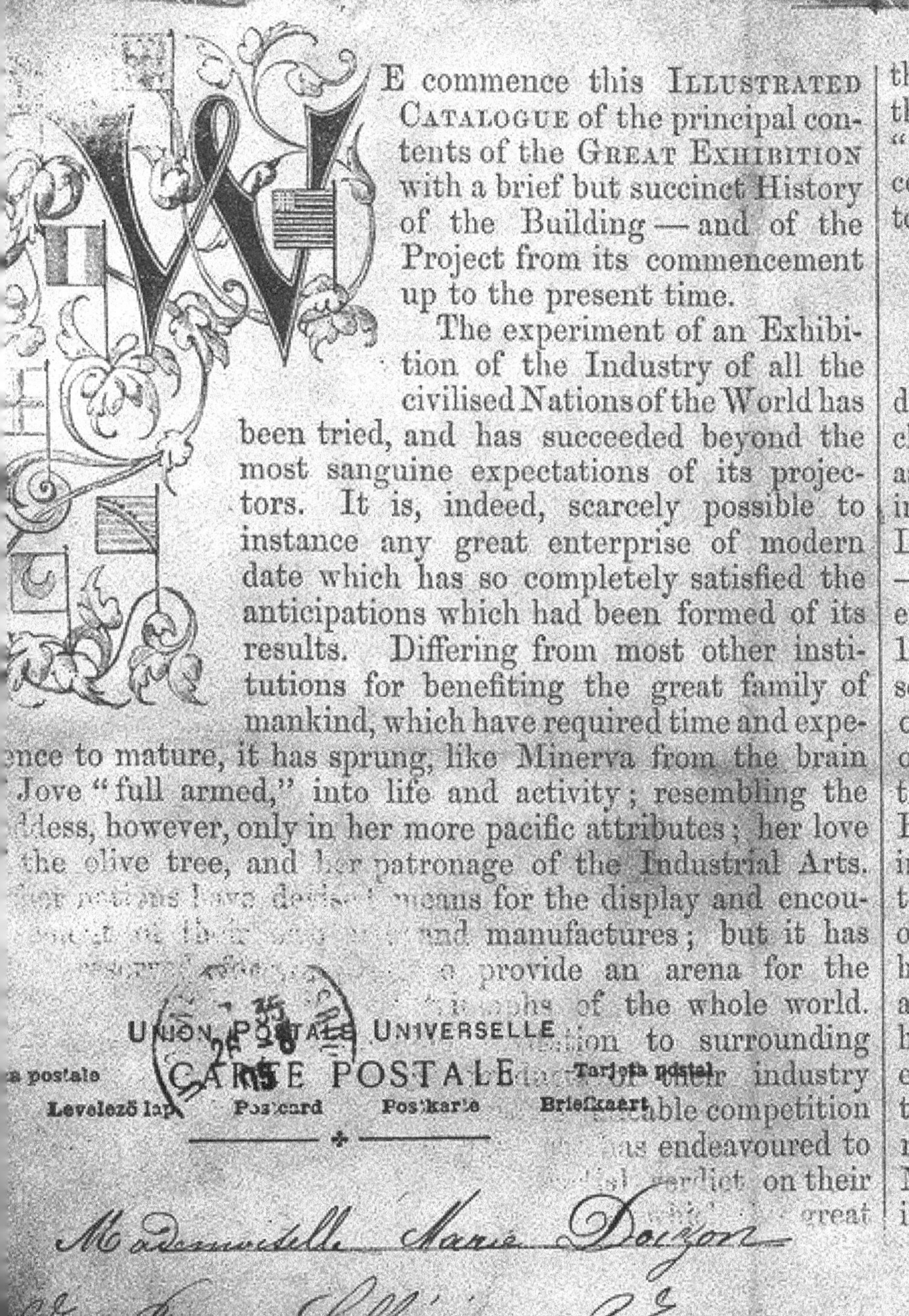

E commence this ILLUSTRATED CATALOGUE of the principal contents of the GREAT EXHIBITION with a brief but succinct History of the Building — and of the Project from its commencement up to the present time.

The experiment of an Exhibition of the Industry of all the civilised Nations of the World has been tried, and has succeeded beyond the most sanguine expectations of its projectors. It is, indeed, scarcely possible to instance any great enterprise of modern date which has so completely satisfied the anticipations which had been formed of its results. Differing from most other institutions for benefiting the great family of mankind, which have required time and expe[ri]ence to mature, it has sprung, like Minerva from the brain [of] Jove "full armed," into life and activity; resembling the [god]dess, however, only in her more pacific attributes; her love [of] the olive tree, and her patronage of the Industrial Arts. [Oth]er nations have devised means for the display and encou[ragement of their commerce] and manufactures; but it has [...] provide an arena for the [... triu]mphs of the whole world. [...] to surrounding [...] their industry [...]able competition [...] endeavoured to [...]al verdict on their [...] great

the prejudices and animosities [...] the happiness of nations; and [...] "peace and good will" which [...] cedents of their prosperity; a[...] told us—

> "Is of the nature [...]
> For then both parties [...]
> And neither party los[...]

It forms no part of our prese[nt] degree of minuteness, into the [...] class; but a brief glance at the [...] associations in France and Eng[land] irrelevant. So far back as 175[...] London offered prizes for speci[...] —tapestry, carpets, porcelain, [...] exhibited the articles which w[...] 1761 and 1762 the artists of[...] selves into two societies for the [...] of art. A few years afterward[s] of Painting was established, [...] the immediate patronage of t[...] Reynolds appointed its Presid[ent] institutions of a similar charact[er] this country, with considerabl[e] of industry they were intende[d] however, be regarded as the or[...] are, in character and plan, most [...] history we are about to enter. [...] essay of Messieurs Challamel a[nd] the Marquis d'Aveze on the su[...] nobleman's appointment to be [...] Manufactories of the Gobe[lins] in 17[...]

Mademoiselle Marie Doizon

Rue Solférino

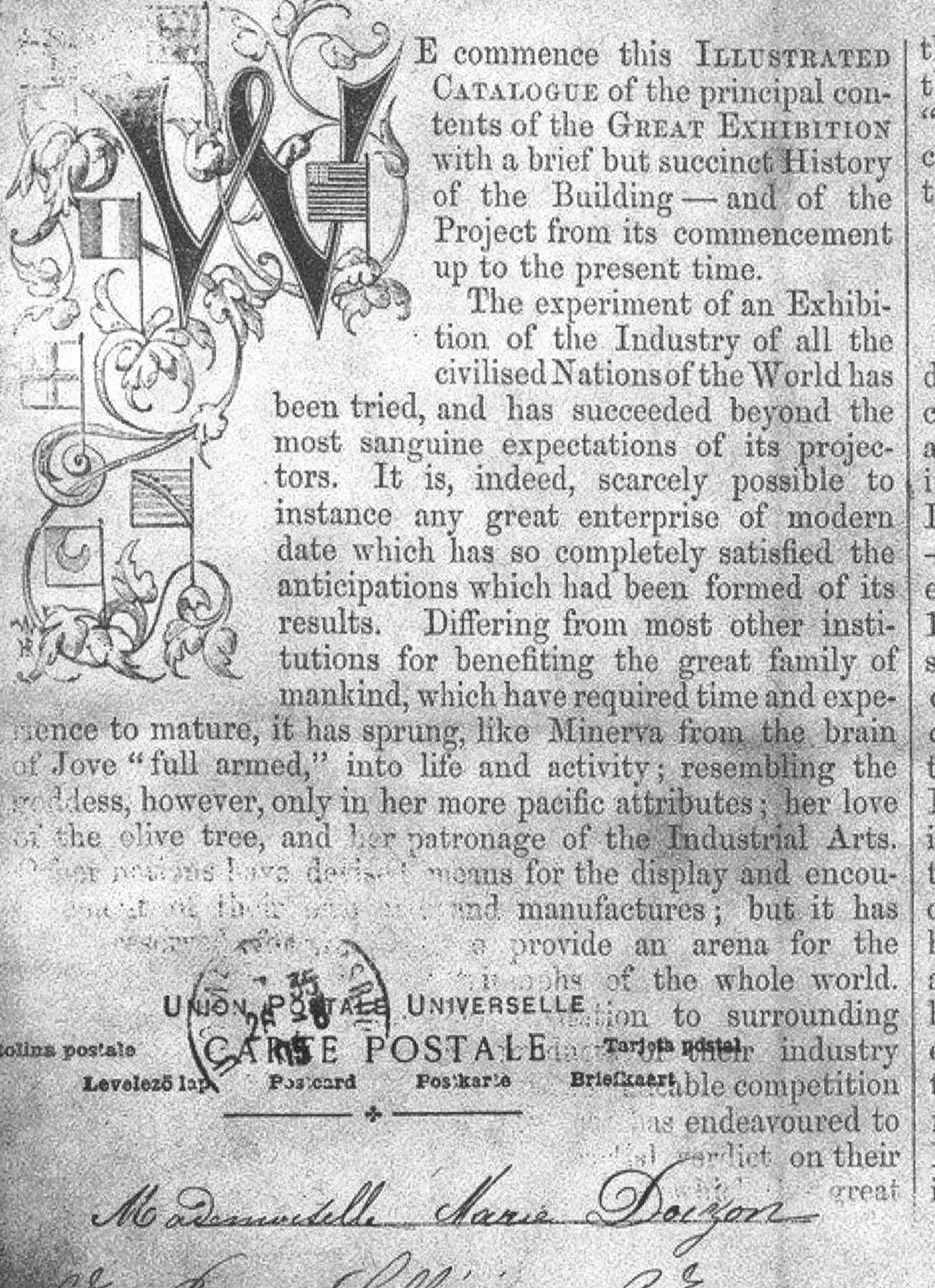

WE commence this ILLUSTRATED CATALOGUE of the principal contents of the GREAT EXHIBITION with a brief but succinct History of the Building — and of the Project from its commencement up to the present time.

The experiment of an Exhibition of the Industry of all the civilised Nations of the World has been tried, and has succeeded beyond the most sanguine expectations of its projectors. It is, indeed, scarcely possible to instance any great enterprise of modern date which has so completely satisfied the anticipations which had been formed of its results. Differing from most other institutions for benefiting the great family of mankind, which have required time and experience to mature, it has sprung, like Minerva from the brain of Jove "full armed," into life and activity; resembling the goddess, however, only in her more pacific attributes; her love of the olive tree, and her patronage of the Industrial Arts. Other nations have devised means for the display and encouragement of their [illegible] and manufactures; but it has [illegible] provide an arena for the [illegible] triumphs of the whole world. [illegible] tion to surrounding [illegible] of their industry [illegible] able competition [illegible] has endeavoured to [illegible] verdict on their [illegible] great

the prejudices and animositi[...] the happiness of nations; a[...] "peace and good will" wh[...] cedents of their prosperity; [...] told us—

> " Is of the nat[...]
> For then both pa[...]
> And neither part[...]

It forms no part of our p[...] degree of minuteness, into t[...] class; but a brief glance at t[...] associations in France and [...] irrelevant. So far back as [...] London offered prizes for sp[...] —tapestry, carpets, porcela[...] exhibited the articles whic[...] 1761 and 1762 the artists [...] selves into two societies for [...] of art. A few years afterw[...] of Painting was establish[...] the immediate patronage o[...] Reynolds appointed its Pr[...] institutions of a similar cha[...] this country, with consider[...] of industry they were inte[...] however, be regarded as th[...] are, in character and plan, n[...] history we are about to ente[...] essay of Messieurs Challam[...] the Marquis d'Aveze on the[...] nobleman's appointment to [...] Manufactories of the Gobel[...] in 17[...]

UNION POSTALE UNIVERSELLE

CARTE POSTALE

Cartolina postale — Tarjeta postal

Levelező lap — Postcard — Postkarte — Briefkaart

Mademoiselle Marie Doizon

9? Place Solferino [illegible]

WE commence this ILLUSTRATED CATALOGUE of the principal contents of the GREAT EXHIBITION with a brief but succinct History of the Building — and of the Project from its commencement up to the present time.

The experiment of an Exhibition of the Industry of all the civilised Nations of the World has been tried, and has succeeded beyond the most sanguine expectations of its projectors. It is, indeed, scarcely possible to instance any great enterprise of modern date which has so completely satisfied the anticipations which had been formed of its results. Differing from most other institutions for benefiting the great family of mankind, which have required time and experience to mature, it has sprung, like Minerva from the brain [of] Jove "full armed," into life and activity; resembling the [go]ddess, however, only in her more pacific attributes; her love [of] the olive tree, and her patronage of the Industrial Arts. [...] means for the display and encou[ragement] [...] and manufactures; but it has [...] provide an arena for the [...] of the whole world. [...] tion to surrounding [...] industry [...] competition [...] endeavoured to [...] verdict on their [...] great

the prejudices and animosities [with] the happiness of nations; and [the] "peace and good will" which [pre]cedents of their prosperity; a[s] told us—

" Is of the nature [...]
For then both parties [...]
And neither party lose[...]

It forms no part of our prese[nt] degree of minuteness, into the [...] class; but a brief glance at the [...] associations in France and Eng[land] irrelevant. So far back as 175[...] London offered prizes for specim[ens] —tapestry, carpets, porcelain, [...] exhibited the articles which w[...] 1761 and 1762 the artists of [them]selves into two societies for the [...] of art. A few years afterward[s] of Painting was established, [...] the immediate patronage of t[he] Reynolds appointed its Presid[ent] institutions of a similar charact[er] this country, with considerable[...] of industry they were intende[d] however, be regarded as the or[...] are, in character and plan, most [...] history we are about to enter. [...] essay of Messieurs Challamel an[d] the Marquis d'Aveze on the su[...] nobleman's appointment to be[...] Manufactories of the Gobelins[...] in 17[...]

Mademoiselle Marie Doizon
[...] Rue Solférino [...]

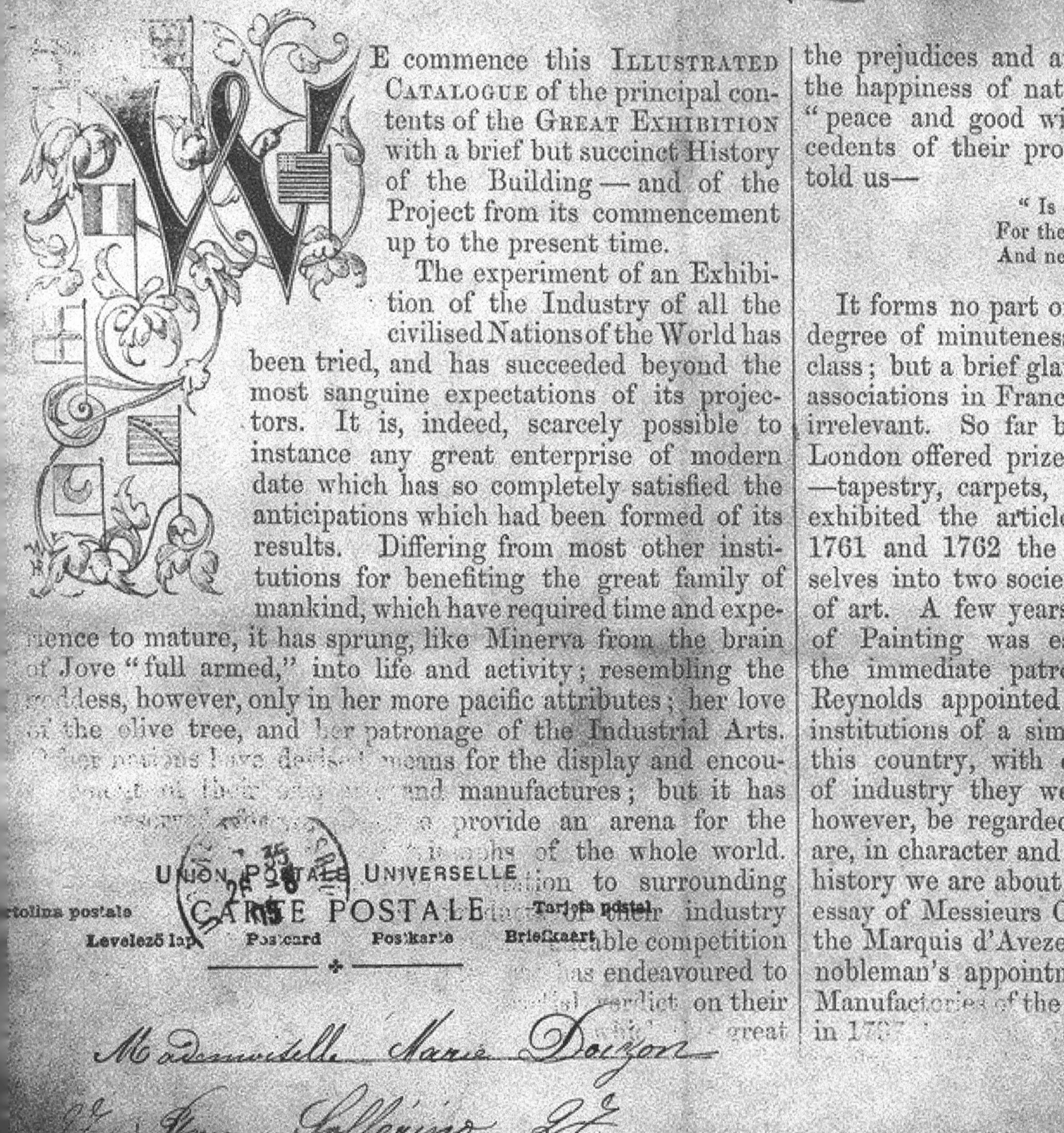

E commence this ILLUSTRATED CATALOGUE of the principal contents of the GREAT EXHIBITION with a brief but succinct History of the Building — and of the Project from its commencement up to the present time.

The experiment of an Exhibition of the Industry of all the civilised Nations of the World has been tried, and has succeeded beyond the most sanguine expectations of its projectors. It is, indeed, scarcely possible to instance any great enterprise of modern date which has so completely satisfied the anticipations which had been formed of its results. Differing from most other institutions for benefiting the great family of mankind, which have required time and experience to mature, it has sprung, like Minerva from the brain of Jove "full armed," into life and activity; resembling the goddess, however, only in her more pacific attributes; her love of the olive tree, and her patronage of the Industrial Arts. Other nations have devised means for the display and encouragement of their commerce and manufactures; but it has been reserved for England to provide an arena for the peaceful triumphs of the whole world. In opposition to surrounding nations, encouraging their industry by the stimulus of favourable competition, England has endeavoured to pass a national verdict on their [...] great

the prejudices and animositi[es ... involve] the happiness of nations; a[nd that] "peace and good will" whi[ch are the antecedents of their prosperity; [... have] told us—

"Is of the nat[ure ...]
For then both par[ties ...]
And neither party [...]"

It forms no part of our p[lan, in any] degree of minuteness, into t[he ...] class; but a brief glance at t[he ...] associations in France and [England is not] irrelevant. So far back as [...] London offered prizes for sp[ecimens of ...] —tapestry, carpets, porcelai[n ...] exhibited the articles whic[h ...] 1761 and 1762 the artists [formed them-] selves into two societies for [the encouragement] of art. A few years afterw[ards the Royal Academy] of Painting was establishe[d, under] the immediate patronage o[f the King;] Reynolds appointed its Pr[esident. The] institutions of a similar cha[racter in] this country, with consider[able ...] of industry they were inte[nded to promote,] however, be regarded as the [...] are, in character and plan, n[ot unlike the] history we are about to ente[r upon. The] essay of Messieurs Challame[l and ...] the Marquis d'Aveze on the [...] nobleman's appointment to [the] Manufactories of the Gobe[lins ...] in 17[...]

To every feather that flies,
Wildering wandering skies,
    For a sigh — Farewell, Adieu?
Sinking suffering heart
That know'st how weary thou art—
    Sore to fain for a flight, —
Aye, spread your wings to depart,
Sad soul and sorrowing heart, —
    Adieu, Farewell, Goodnight.

Adieu.

Weary whispering trees,
What do you say to the breeze?
    And what says the breeze to you?
With passing [illegible] its own [illegible],
Murm'ring murmuring trees,
    Would ye [illegible] our Adieus?
Topping [illegible]
Wraith that [illegible] with these,
    Echo heard in the [illegible], —
[illegible] fleeting life ill at [illegible]

In every flake that flies,
Wildering wandering skies,
    For a sigh — Farewell, Adieu?
Sinking suffering heart
That know'st how weary thou art —
    Soul so fain for a flight, —
Aye, spread your wings to depart,
Sad soul and sorrowing heart, —
    Adieu, Farewell, Goodnight.

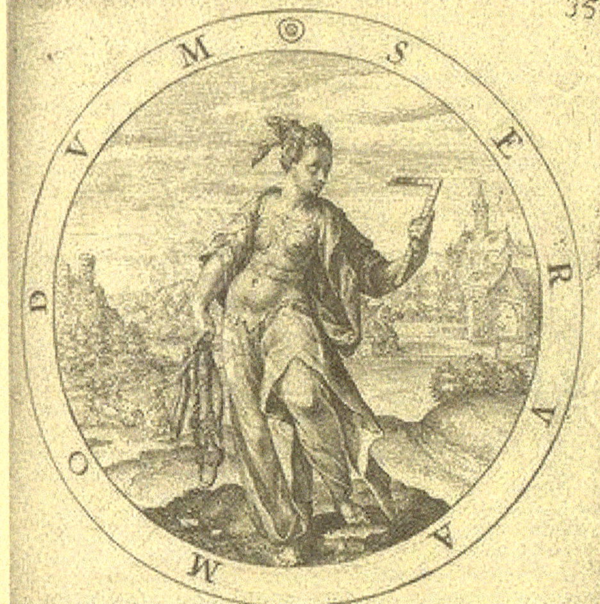

Mens servare modum, rebus sufflata secundis,
Nescit, & affectus frena tenere sui

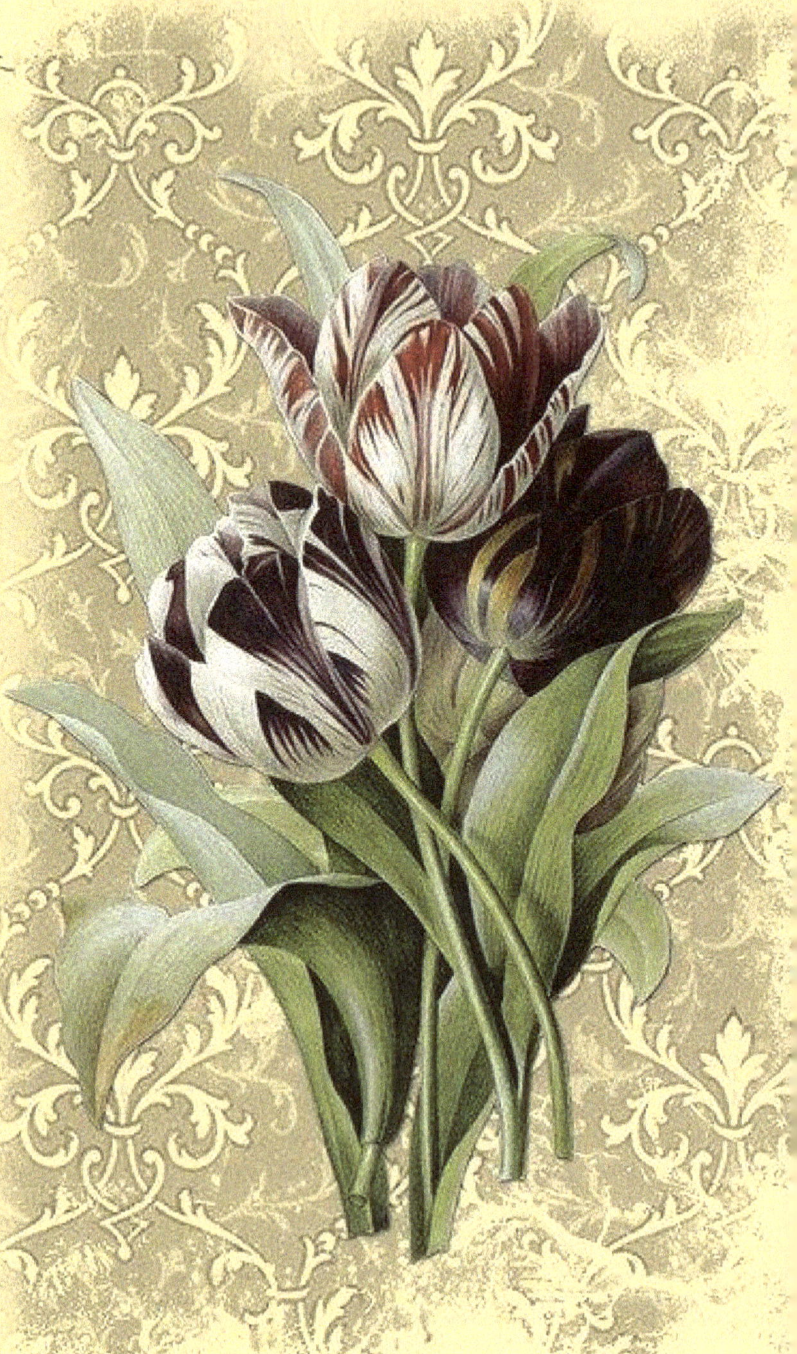

Adieu.

Weary whispering trees,
What do you say to the breeze,
    And what says the breeze to you?
And passing shells all at ease,
Merrily murmuring trees,
    Would ye longer linger au Adieu?
Tossing turbulent seas,
Winds that wrestle with these,
    Echo heard in the dell, —
And fleeting life ill at ease

PARIS... EN FLANANT
La Tour Eiffel

POUR CAR
METTEZ
L'ARRONDISSE

PARIS... EN FLANANT

Le Tour Eiffel

POUR CAR
METTEZ
L'ARRONDISSEM

I.B.C. 0628

PARIS... EN FLANANT

La Tour Eiffel

POUR PAR
METTEZ
L'ARRONDISSE

C. 0628

PARIS... EN FLANANT
La Tour Eiffel
POUR PAR
METTEZ
L'ARRONDISSEM